AF583161

"So whether you eat or drink, or whatever you do,
do all to the glory of God." (1 Co 10:31)

ISBN: 978-607-29-5918-7

Originally published in Spanish, December 2020.
First reprint in September 2023.
First English edition September 2024.

This book belongs to:

____

To Catalina, Mariana, Jorge David and Elisa.

My Christmas Gift

Ana Sofia Azcunaga Lozano
Jorge Jose Montemayor Cantu

Do you want to hear about a *fun* tradition in my family?

Every year we get ready for Christmas by decorating our house. Our place looks amazing and festive. Setting everything up is a family activity.

We put colorful string lights outside,

a Christmas tree in the living room,

ornaments, stockings, candles, jingle bells...

... and many other decorations!

Do you know which one is my favorite?
The nativity scene! With
Our Mother Mary, Saint Joseph, and
Baby Jesus lying in the manger.

My parents say that the most
important thing about Christmas is
that Jesus is born, bringing
love, peace and joy to our hearts.

Another thing that I
really look forward to is
presents!

Every year I work on a special
gift for Jesus that I make
from the bottom
of my heart.

This year my birthday present
for Baby Jesus will be:

I wish I could go meet Jesus and give him my gift. I will share this idea with my mom. I think she will like it very much.

"Mom: can we go to the place where Jesus was born? I would like to see him and give him my present."

My mom smiled at me and said: "That would be lovely! But Bethlehem is very far away from here and I don't know how to get there."

Luckily, my dad was listening, and he knew how to get there!

"If we want to visit Jesus at the stable where he is, we have to follow the star of Bethlehem. It is the brightest star in the sky," he said.

I jumped up in excitement and ran outside to look for the star. Finding it was easy because of its sparkling light. We got in the car and started our journey.

The road was long, and so was our drive. But we were

never lost, because the Star of Bethlehem guided our way and soon we arrived at the stable.

We got out of the car and the first thing I saw was St. Joseph coming to greet us.

He said: "Welcome! Thank you for coming! Would you like to meet my family? Jesus, Mary, our friends are here!" St. Joseph is very kind and has a gentle smile. He gathered hay bales for us to sit comfortably, what a nice host!

I ran to Our Mother Mary with my arms wide open and she gave me a big long hug.

She loves me so much.

She said to me: "Jesus is here for you!" Jesus is the most precious baby I have ever seen. He looked into my eyes and giggled. My heart felt so happy.

I asked Our Mother Mary:

"May I hold your baby?"

She was touched and said yes.

She lifted him out of the manger and carefully placed him in my arms. She showed me how to hold him.

I really enjoyed my special moment holding Baby Jesus...

...and he did too!

Suddenly I remembered his present and said: "Jesus, I am so happy for your birth, and I brought a gift that I have been working on with much love for you."

Baby Jesus was happy, and Mary seemed pleased about it.

Our Mother Mary told me something very important: "Jesus also has a gift for you. He is here to show you the way to Heaven."

She told me how Jesus would stay with me, in my heart, to look after me, so that someday we can live forever with them in Heaven.

Jesus gave me the most special present I will ever receive. It is something that I will cherish and care for every day. I want to be close to Jesus always.

"Would you like to stay for dinner?" St. Joseph asked. "Our friends, the shepherds, brought us some food."

We felt very excited and grateful to receive this invitation, and sat down to eat. We had bread, cheese, and fruit. Our Christmas dinner at home is delicious and fun, but this one was perfect!

Thank you Holy Family

for the best Christmas ever! Thanks for having

us in your stable, for my special gift, and

for bringing Jesus into the world!

www.ingramcontent.com/pod-product-compliance
Lightning Source LLC
LaVergne TN
LVHW071131160826
845679LV00005B/1247
9786072959187